Echocs III
Even More Neo-Victorian Poetry

by

JaniceT

ISBN: 1537189751
ISBN-13: 9781537189758

Acknowledgments

I am deeply indebted to the following people. Dover Whitecliff, author of The Stolen Songbird, wanted to know what had become of the captain and crew of the "other ship" in "Airship" in Echoes ll. There would be no "Dragon" without her. Belinda and Anthony Sykes helped greatly with editing. Mary Louder, my gregarious friend, is the explicit inspiration for But Mary Does. The Metaphor 3 writer's group, and it's curator, Ronald Peat, made gracious and insightful suggestions on my work. I'm also indebted to Stanley Thompson, who's candor and knowledge help to shape my work. Emily Thompson, author of the Clockwork Twist adventure series, designed the interior and cover of this book, as well as the formatting.

Thank you, each and all, ever so much!

- Index -

But Mary Does...9

The Hobo Code...10

Doubtless...13

Like a Shallow Grave...15

Indisposed..17

Airship (Part 1)..18

Dragon (Part 2)..20

One Thing That I Possess......................................23

Such Gifts...25

The Nurture of Nature..27

Pluviophile..29

When Sunlight Fails...31

Longings..33

Piratess...34

The Medicine We're Taking....................................37

Upon a Road 39

Cancer Dancers..41

A Kind Word Shared...43

Dogmatism..45

Heaven's Muse..47

Casualty..49

Morpheus..51

A Gentle Jostle...53

Missing..55

Addiction..57

Nightfall...59

But Mary Does

We're chatting in a small cafe
Where windows keep the gray at bay
And as I answer with a shout
The hiding Sun comes bursting out
As though on cue and so we laugh
No other patron gets our gaff,
But Mary does.

A story that is often told
Is easily dismissed as old
No longer fit to entertain
Or even countered with disdain.
So few will once more hear that tale
With interest, and smile as well,
But Mary does.

Then by the jilted clock we spy,
That several hours have sped by
With total disregard of we
Who could have bantered endlessly.
I know not many who would stay
To talk an afternoon away,
But Mary does.

The Hobo Code

A knocking on the door frame.
"Ma'am, you got any chores?"
She sends him, with instructions, to the barn,

Then to her kitchen scurries
To stir the stew once more
Sweet biscuits in the oven keeping warm.

Her husband home and tired.
A day of labor spent.
He notices the table set for three.

Just as the lonely drifter
His head bent in respect
Reports that he is bidden to come eat.

A thankful grace is offered
Then dishes passed around
The husband asks the drifter how he knew

That he would meet no trouble
When coming to their door
The neighbors being contrary and rude.

He points out towards the fence post
Says that he read the sign
Etched there for every vagabond to know.

The couple, clearly baffled
The drifter smiles to say
Some hobo came before and left the code.

JaniceT

It indicated "Friendly,"
That work and food were here.
The other fences warned to steer away.

So, up and down the byways
As drifters tend to roam
They know where aid, or tribulation, lay.

Doubtless

Doubtless there is more to say
Of love than Shakespeare knew
More images to pen and paint
Than Albrecht Durer drew
And stars still to be counted when
Copernicus was through
Much more by far from sea to star
When humans dare to do.

Doubtless Bach did not exhaust
The prelude and the fugue
Nor Tesla eek out all there was
From his electric muse
Or Groves foresee the cost now reaped
Of Oppenheimer's fuse
As is the nature of such things
Which humans dare to do

Doubtless there is more to tour
of Armstrong's gentle Moon
And fathoms deep as yet to reach
Than Cousteau could pursue
Now planet-wide computers thrive
in pockets old and new
Till I implore, "Just how much more
Will humans dare to do?"

Like a Shallow Grave

Why am I doomed to this,
A shallow grave?
Why die I waiting for
The muse to write,
Anticipating movement
Deep within,
Perchance to resurrect
And reunite
With winds diaphanous,
With waves of light?
With burning, purging passion
Dance I there
Caught up between fulfillment
And despair,
Then winding down and rounded
To a dirge.
So does this one compose
Mid grope and cling
And only while the muse
Is yet in sight.
Alas, her visage dims.
Again my plight.
I lapse into this grave and
Wait to write.

Indisposed

Entrenched behind a narrow desk,
Which faces out against the glass,
She labors on the internet
As timeless hours amble past.

Covertly glancing at the view
She hides behind her tilted blinds
And so her neighbors also do.
Computers on, in joint disguise.

She never leaves, and doesn't care
Beyond the confines of her room
But for the parcels that will bare
Against her door each afternoon.

A gentle tap arouses her
Then footsteps softly pad away.
The neighbors have already stirred
To seize their orders for the day.

And so it goes for she and those
Who share this solitary cast
Content to pose as indisposed
As timeless hours amble past.

Airship
Part 1

How far I've flown I neither know nor care.
Much as this open deck my plans are bare.
Of star or compass I have nary need,
But follow as these downy cloud tops lead.

The chilly breezes toying through my hair
Cascade across my skin and jacket flare
While on the bottoms of my booted feet
The engine taps an unrelenting beat.

I acquiesce to gentle bob and sway
Beneath balloon and rigging bloated shape.
Awaiting now the nearly risen sun
I scan the vast expanse and see no one.

And yet, I hear a rumbling of some sort
Then luminescing clouds off to my port
Combusting deep with ever brighter tones
Now booming louder, louder, nearer, NO!

Bombastic airship, cannons bursting now,
Ejected straight at me from out its shroud.
A maniac, that pilot, heaving hard
Just missing our collision by one yard.

His tortured face, the horror in those eyes,
For near destroying me, so I surmised,
Until I saw his passing stern ablaze.
Then mammoth winged beast in brutal chase

JaniceT

Erupting, fierce and howling, scales agleam.
The hot concussion of its down-spent wing
That final moment as it thrust away
Forced ship and I and all the world to sway.

Then came the screams, the pounding and a moan
As crew and cargo floundered down below
Caught in the violent swinging disarray.
The flaming ship and dragon sped away

To disappear in yet another cloud.
Our vessel's motion finally calmed down.
Those lightly injured put the ship aright,
And unspilled rum was quickly spent that night.

Now star and compass were of urgent need
This damaged vessel and the injuries
Required that we find a ready port
Equipped to lend us aid of every sort.

I searched in haste upending fore and aft
For sextant, compass, and the proper map,
Then finally we found the guiding star
And made for help that wasn't very far.

By dawn I bid the floating docks goodbye
With only half a crew and resupply
But, now where'er I travel through the sky
I keep the navigation tools nearby.

Echoes III

Dragon
Part 2

All cannons spent, and rudder full aflame
He pulls well hard upon the wheel and cranes
A sweat-drenched brow around to quickly spy
How close they're being followed through the sky.

So close! He thrusts the wheel to push away
The beast would give no quarter to its prey.
Up through the clouds they flew to buy some time,
But nearly hit an airship passing by.

Oh how the startled captain of that ship
Had fought to veer before his vessel flipped
And tumbled out of view, just when, below,
Through thinning cloud the sea begins to show

So down to that abyss he aims the bow
The crew holds fast. It's only seconds now.
The captain heaves the wheel, the stern slams hard
Torrential plumes of water now bombard

The dragon's groping jaws, engulfed, and gone,
Then thrashing to survive with all it's brawn
While captain, ship, and crew fly well away.
The fires are out, but damages remain.

Then, all becalmed, they each began to ask
What could have spurred that creature to attack.
They'd happened on it's cavern unaware
For on that very spot the charts were bare.

JaniceT

They'd had to swerve to miss it very near.
A subtle bump and they were in the clear
And off they'd hurried, loot-less, knowing well
That none who plunders dragons live to tell.

Then out of nowhere one great beastial cry
Had everybody staring eye to eye.
A second later all the crew aboard
Ran to a cannon, blunderbuss, or sword.

And yet, it was the captain's frenzied skill
Which served to save them all from being killed.
Now each was pressed to mending everything
From makeshift rudder to pectoral wings.

By morning they had managed to regain
Their charted course, though weary and in pain.
In shifts they rested, eager to see port.
How fortunate this trip was fairly short.

Soon, as they disembarked their tethered ship,
Which, floating on soft breezes, bobbed a bit,
A passing stevedore stopped short and stared
At something underneath the vessel where

It seemed to him that something shiny lodged.
The captain looked, and sadly knew what caused
That dragon's rabid chase and anguished wails;
The keel was now embedded with it's scales.

Echoes III

JaniceT

One Thing That I Possess

There is within my heart and mind
One thing that I possess
It is the very dear desire
To nurture dreams and love inspire
To bring you happiness.

And though at times it may appear
I own but courser stuff
The moment I perceive your need
Away are banished anger, greed
All forces raw and rough.

So each new day and evening
I'm eager that you know
How very dear you are to me
That your regard does intercede
And bid me tell you so.

Such Gifts

The flowers that he brings me are not garden grown,
Nor standing in a pretty vase for all to see,
And yet, their scent, the sweetest that has ever blown,
Wafts through each loving kindness that he spends on me,

And oh the rich confections that he ever brings,
Presented without shiny wrap or showy bows,
Reside within his effortlessly humble deeds
Until my very heart no other flavor knows.

Each thoughtful, loving act inspires me to show
That not one of his precious gifts goes without heed,
Nor would I trade sweet chocolate or the balmy rose
For all the loving kindnesses he spends on me.

The Nurture of Nature

Guard well this tender cradle.
In every aspect strive
To nurture as you're able
That you and all may thrive.

Be not in haste to gamble
This rich estate away
On promises of ample
Enrichments to be made.

No matter how beguiling
Scorn negligence and greed.
This is your bed and bounty
Your very life, indeed.

Guard well this tender cradle
For Nature, like a host,
Will set an ample table
For those who prize it most.

Pluviophile

I pull the curtains back
From windows clear and wide
In earnest, hopeful stance
To search the open sky
For merest wisp of cloud
In arcing ever blue
Until I burst aloud,
"The rain is long past due!"

Where is that swollen scent
When sea birds fill the air
And moisture not yet spent
Is lurking everywhere.
Why do they stay away,
This season's will defy?
Oh how I miss those days
When all the sky would cry.

When Sunlight Fails

When everywhere seems clouded gloom,
When disappointments press,
A famine of the heart presumes
That every joy is less

No matter gentle pleasantries
Nor comforting caress
Nor any offered remedy
To someone so depressed.

Yet, ample joys there'll always be
To tug the sunken chest
Until what seemed sheer misery
Proves but a little test.

Longings

As if a cave could, screaming, yawn and grope
With every hope of filling empty spaces
This room within my flesh, my womb, cries out
For those fulfillments of a child's traces
Along the inner walls in search of faces.

As if an ocean tide were beckoning
While pulling me unhindered through the foam
Eroding wave by wave my chance to flee
And join with reason on a shore of stone
A yearning to conceive now draws me home.

As if, amid a forest I've been roaming,
A broad, bright meadow flashes into sight
Where never was a meadow to my knowing
Maternal longings seize with sudden might
My body in a permeating light.

Piratess

She knew her way around the timbered decks
The weft and weave and mendings of each sail.
Her father, stalwart pirate born and bred,
A widower, or so was told the tale.

But for one port, at sea throughout the year,
Aboard a frigate, haven, classroom, home.
And so she grew without the slightest fear
In all things that a pirate ought to know.

The warmth of rum had early passed her lips
For shipboard water unto spoilage tends.
She feasted on provisions from such ships
As drew within the telescopic lens.

Her uncles, pirates all, at daylight's end
Told lively yarns: the exploits of their youth.
She smiled, and laughed, and ventured to pretend
That she was none too savvy of the truth.

In time she grew to be a winsome maid
Quite capable, robust, and worldly wise.
In all things she was fiercely unafraid
And spoke her heart with no hint of device.

In clashes, ship to ship, she held her own
Regarding each engagement, closely fought,
As opportunity to test and hone
While sizing up potential pirate stock.

JaniceT

One day an able seaman joined the crew,
Survivor of a battle dearly won,
Belligerent, at first, until he proved
That he would be a lackey to no one.

Intrigued, she slowly dropped her guard, which led
To something of a charismatic spell
That snared them both, and in due time they wed;
A peerless match, or so was told the tale.

JaniceT

The Medicine We're Taking

Every spoonful is inclined
To dull the senses, bind the mind.
Beneath its candy coating find
The medicine we're taking.
Its every gram is time released
Extending our synthetic peace.
Though human problems seldom cease
There can be no mistaking
The power in this tiny pill
That quiets every thought and will
Unless one is immune or ill
Affected, thus forsaking.
Forsaken, then, as beasts unfit
Are those who do not swallow it
But heed a violent urge to spit
The medicine we're taking.

JaniceT

Upon a Road

I can no longer see it now,
That road I would have traveled down
If you and I had not divinely met
Along those busy avenues
Which everyone was want to use.
I might have just continued on, and yet,
Once we engaged, as by design,
Just long enough to redefine
The rigid steps that I was set to make.
Then, timid strides in unison
Evolved, and now we walk as one
Upon a road that only we can take.

JaniceT

Cancer Dancers

Where smokestack fumes
Melt into rain cloud skies,
Where life between the
Toxic layer dies,
Where man's cacophony
Goes unabated,
To hound the ear
With hummed vibrations dated,
Where minds lie steeped
In phosphorescent tubes,
Where plastic proteins
Pose as staple foods,
Where spirits break
Beneath an axe of taxes,
Where rules of conduct
Vie for vulgar maxims,
Where people as an
Acrid cancer spread
All virtues of this Earth
Are rendered dead.

A Kind Word Shared

He seemed to one auspicious purpose born:
As antidote to those who droop forlorn.
His ever conscious kindnesses renewed
Forgotten hopes, and cheerfulness imbued.

A kind word shared with one whose dour mien
Would otherwise illicit mute disdain
Slow melted even those of hardened heart
Who found no shred of malice on his part.

Of income he had but enough to live
Yet never would rebuff a chance to give.
He held no vented slights of any sort
But always lent, of others, good report.

His gentleness and caring manner proved
Sweet remedy to those who would be soothed
Alas, I only knew him passively
Yet, he's the sort of person I would be.

JaniceT

Dogmatism

He asked of my opinion on
The world and what I thought was wrong.
I gave him that I didn't know
And from that point he'd not let go
But gripped me firm upon the arm
Thus, I was sure he meant me harm.
My heart felt like it up and ran.
I didn't even know the man
Who barked out some dogmatic speech
And on and on and on he preached.
His face appeared to change just then,
Some sort of transformation, when
I glanced back to his hand and saw,
Instead of human flesh, a paw.
My startled eyes resumed the face.
His ears began to point and raise.
His features whirled into a blur.
Regaining focus all was fur.
Instead of nose or thin lipped mouth
There issued from his face a snout
Beneath two great brown, rounded eyes
While all the while he barked and cried
And howled and scratched at fur and flea.
I managed then my arm to free
And lunged in terror through the door.
I'll habitate that place no more
But now admit I never heard,
Of that which he proclaimed, one word.

Heaven's Muse

The muse who whispers in my ear
Must from bright Heaven come to light
Upon my shouldered hair

And there to cling with tiny hands
To swirling strands of golden tress
And, cooing, bid me write.

She lends a mood unto my mind
And I am long inclined to hear
Her every murmured sound

As blunted words grow round and soft
And form an image of those scenes
Which only we can see.

JaniceT

Casualty

Woman, turn your tearing eyes
The rabble have betrayed you,
Lied to you and compromised
Your femininity.

Little did you realize
What you were being led to.
Dramatized and victimized
You are a casualty.

Gone, that clime before my time,
When morals were of value,
When rules complied to codify
Imbued propriety.

Those opposed to this arose
In ever greater volume.
Alas, the blind constrain the guide,
To your calamity.

JaniceT

Morpheus

Sweet Morpheus, envelop me in dreams
Come guide me gently from these feral schemes
That convolute my poorly sorted brain
Till I arise and pace the floor again.
Fatiguing all the more this body spent
This tortured soul as grief will not relent
To lie on linen bathed in moonlight beams
Sweet Morpheus, envelop me in dreams.

A Gentle Jostle

A gentle jostle wakes me from my musings
Just as a depot jerks, then slides away.
Confusion screams, "What station was I viewing?
How long my stupor? Have I overstayed?"
Frenetic lurch in search of a conductor,
Or anyone who knows just where we are.
Unsteady, stumble, fall, then I remember;
My ticket will not take me very far.
I struggle to my feet as others glower
And bring my sore arm up to read my watch,
But no! In haste to meet them in one hour
My wallet and my timepiece were forgot.
And since my frugal nature so beguiled
I'd carried just enough to board the train.
Now comes the terse conductor down the aisle
To scan our vouchers. All is now in vain!
"Your ticket, sir?" he asks, and I awaken
To meet his pithy stare and upturned palm.
A gentle jostle as we leave the station
As I relax anew, and yawn, becalmed.

Missing

Reaching for the gravy ladle,
Ready to consume,
A golden turkey, mashed potatoes,
Yams and stuffing, too.
Each bona fide Thanksgiving staple
Lavishly in view.
But something that my memories cradle
Says this isn't true,
For, what is missing at our table
Is, quite plainly, you.
One day, when everyone is able,
When can we resume
Our long tradition, tried and stable,
We will feast anew.

Addiction

Two hands clasped round my head
Another plunged into my chest
Cradling my heart.
They pull with mammoth force
While I, possessed of neither mind nor will,
Am dragged a steady pace
Into a space forbidden
And I am lost.
The sirens call, of drink or drug
Or any medium they choose,
Breed sweet prismatic sounds
'Till I forget to breath
And am received by Death's dark,
hungry, hollow hounds.

Nightfall

Deep, deep within these pages
A cherished, careworn tome
I scarcely feel the ages
Of hours I've been home
Nor notice I the rhythm
The tick of tocking gears
Until the soft collision
When chimes invade my ears
It's ten now by the counting
So close the book, alas,
To stretching yawning frowning
That so much time has passed
Lethargically I struggle
Lift all my tired weight
Then to my bed I shuffle
To dreams I can't abate
Oh wait! The clock needs winding
And have I locked the door?
The will is yet aspiring
But I can do no more
Than quietly surrender
Into my bed I fall
And hope that I remembered
The clock, the door and all.

~~ Thank you ~~

If you are interested in finding more information
about the poetry of JaniceT, visit her blog at:
janice-t.weebly.com

Also Available:
Echoes: Neo-Victorian Poetry (2013)
Echoes II: More Neo-Victorian Poetry (2014)